Testimony of Miracle

Hope Jean Stewart

WORKBOOK PRESS LLC
187 E Warm Springs Rd,
Suite B285 Las Vegas NV 89119 USA

Website: https://workbookpress.com/
Hotline: 1-888-818-4856
Email: admin@workbookpress.com

Ordering Information:

Quantity sales. Special discounts are available on quantity purchases by corporations, associations, and others. For details, contact the publisher at the address above.

Library of Congress Control Number:

ISBN-13:   978-1-963718-69-0   Paperback Version
                978-1-963718-70-6   Digital Version

REV. DATE: 06/13/2024

Other Book by Hope Stewart

HELLFIRE IS REAL

Hellfire is Real, has been truly insightful, and reached the heart of many.

I feel grateful to have Had the opportunity to touch lives, in such a special way.

TABLE OF CONTENTS

ABOUT THE AUTHOR – THAT'S ME!

I have lived in the United Kingdom, where I have spent most of my life. My father and I, were part of the wind rush generation in the 1940s. There was a period, when Britain needed help from their closest allies, to restore the state after the second world war. I was young then, with no thought of what the future will hold, or who I would truly become. I just take life as it comes. Living in the United Kingdom has shaped my life, and to an extent, the person I am today. And I will always be immensely grateful for the wonderful effects. This does not mean life was, or even near perfect! As it really never is, no matter who and where you are. Life is designed to live, but live and learn through diverse experiences. Life is also quite mysterious, in the way these experiences somehow, guide you to where you should be, at different stages...

Being born and bred in the beautiful Caribbean island of Jamaica – the place I truly called home! It is simply the only magnificent place, that totally grips my heart entirely. And for sure, I would not deliberate on the less than great side of Jamaica, because there is much more greatness, to spend my time reminiscing over. Jamaica's beauty and true sense of community spirit, give generously to why is it so special. It is almost like natural force of nature, that continuously pulls you under its luscious canopy – I meant this in the most positive and exciting way. Jamaica being my queen of heart, It is always at the fore front of my mind – the reason, I would visit whenever there is an opportunity... I believe one day, it might be my home again – to enjoy a great sense of nature, relaxation, and all year – round sunshine. I missed that, great deal! And for sure, I have

1

not forgotten about mother nature, that it is prone to some serious natural disasters, but so is everywhere else on the planet. Home is where the heart is, as the saying goes.

Aside from my spiritual and personable nature, I can acknowledge my constant urge and enthusiasm to help, care and support others. This aspect of my personality, I appreciate always, but never more so, than when it led me to the path of health and social care. I spent many years working in the health field. It is a tremendous area of work – through not without its rewards and drawbacks. Being able to contribute positively and effectively, to the lives of those who trust us to take care of them, is a phenomenal opportunity. This is never truer than now, as our world is debilitated with the incredible paralytic and deadly covid 19. An amazing stagnant time, emotionally, physically, and definitely mentally. For many health care workers who are able to share their stories, it may bring forth a sense of gratitude – knowing, they have not been conquered by coronavirus, whilst giving

Despite millions died from covid 19, there are more survivals – thank God for that!!! Some may say it is a miracle they are still alive, after came so closed to dying. I have not heard anyone who were unconscious, and on the brink of taking their last breath said, it is pure coincidence I am still alive. In fact, even those who perhaps did not believe in miracles before, believe in it after such extremely traumatic experience. However, it is not the case, where miracle is the only reason millions of covid 19 sufferers survived – this is also down other factors, such as care. But listening to survivors covid 19 journeys, it is hard to not see the role, miracle plays in their recovery. On many occasions, miracles happen quite openly for others to see, although not always the case. But it is great when its occurrence is obvious – as seeing is believing. Open miracle is not a modern thing - historically, Jesus did these on many occasions. Jesus humbly commits himself unconditionally to helping, healing, and aiding people's needs – and he used his supernatural power, to work miracles then, and still now.

Bottomline is life is a journey, and I am grateful for my time. Fulfilling my purpose in life, is my primary mission – especially, where my spiritual life is concerns. I am happy and contented with my spiritual life, and hopefully will create the overall life balance, I am working towards. I am tremendously grateful for the ability to continuously learn and aspire, as I travel my life journey. Knowledge is that blanket we all need, to help us through … It is the power tool, we should always have in our pockets wherever we go, or whatever we do.

I hope sharing aspects of my life has enlightened, and given insight into my world.

Hope stewart

DEDICATION

This book is dedicated to some amazing people, who have hugely contributed to my life.

Some were my constant 'go to' and other are still my rock. They have lifted me up, in ways no other did. They understood my life challenges, and provided guidance in very special ways. I know how privileged I am, to have them in my life. I quite often feel, they brought tremendous wealth (not financial wealth) to my world, and made my life journey worthwhile.

Now it is my honour, to say Thank you. And remind them, just how precious and priceless, they are.

Special Thanks to my special son, Wayne Stewart Joseph, my mother Mrs. Olga Small- Williams, my father Alfred Stewart, my great grandmother Mrs. Eliza Ricketts, my grand Aunt Margret Ricketts, my grand uncle Mr. John Ricketts, my grand uncle Mr. James Ricketts, my grand Aunt Conda Ricketts. To the Henry and the Godelia families.

To all my siblings Ellen, George, Mary, and Trevor to all my nieces and nephews.

A very special thank you acknowledgement to the following people. Miss Karlene Mitchell, Mrs. Marjorie Kennedy, Mrs. Leonie Walcott and Miss Pauline Edwards, and a special thanks to Miss Melrose White for everything. God's blessing on you all.

Once again I would like to give a special acknowledgement to Mrs. Marjorie Kennedy, who God use to tell me, to write this book in 2016.

May God continue to bless and keep you all. My heart will always be a place, where love, loyalty and sincerity abide, for you.

Testimony of Miracle

PREFACE

Testimony of miracles, is about the miracles God has done in my life, and in the life. It will highlight my journeys, real experiences, and supernatural outcomes of some extenuating circumstances.

My experiences are all different, through as connected me closer to God and to my faith.

Each of my personal testimonies, help me to acknowledge the importance of my faith, in Jesus Christ. As it is through faith, we can accept and understand the depth of miracles. These testimonies are phenomenally empowering, and utterly inspirational.

Miracles are based on the manifestation of God's power. It is safe to say, not only are we capable of experiencing miracles in our daily lives, but everything about our existence, is on the premise of miracle. God makes miracles happen for us, but we are incapable of performing miracles. Should mankind be able to do what God does, then we could abolish the concepts of miracle boundaries of medicine, alongside many other phenomenal apparatuses. Yet, there are many significant things, humans will never be able to do. For instance, we have no control over time, or anything that is naturally occurring, for that matter. And this is because we are not God, and do not have the supernatural power of miracle – humans lack, real influential effects, in this respect.

Being able to share from the premise of miracle, is a tremendous blessing. It is my belief, many people are waiting to hear more about God, as they have not yet the full understanding of his history and existence in our lives – and most of all, his spiritual impact on our experiences.

It is without a doubt, that many people experienced miracles in their daily lives. This occurrence may be just once, or even on multiple occasions – there are no stipulations, as to who when, and how many times someone can, or will experience special miracle, throughout their lives. This is so, regardless of whether people acknowledge these experiences as miracles, mere coincidences, or just good luck. Miracles are extraordinary, unexpected occurrences, which would not happen under normal circumstances. They are not generally explainable, with the application of science or natural laws. Miracles are attributed through divine power – God almighty.

Understanding the differentiation between miracles and coincidences, is fantastic. It helps to make clear the distinction between natural laws and God's laws.

I accept, some people may not see miracles through the same religious spectacles, as I do. Different religious group may have varied views on miracles – and others, may not have a perception at all. Or it may be the case, where some people's idea of miracle, is that it does not exist, or it is flawed occurrences. I am fairly certain, there are other many varied explanations …

However, for me, the experience of miracles, eradicate all dismissal against its occurrence. I trust everyone who reads these books, will become more spiritually aware. And have an understanding, of the extremity of God's work in our lives – the work of miracles.

It is long established deep in the biblical history; Jesus Christ is a miracle worker. And today, he is still working miracles. To be accepting of God laws, is to acknowledge the existence of miracles, without limitations.

Do you believe in miracle?

Would you like a miracle?

What would you like it to be?

What would it mean to you, to have a miracle?

Have you ever experienced miracles?

Have your miracles ever touched the lives of others?

How or what way, your miracle story impacted the lives of others?

LET US KEEP OUR LIVES FRAME WITH THE GRACE OF GOD, THAT OUR MIRACLES MAY BE PRESENT, IN THE TIME OF NEEDS.

THERE IS ALWAYS TIME FOR A MIRACLE.

There is something extraordinary about sharing – especially sharing personal experiences, which Are deeply touching. This may be because it reflects real situations, rather than exaggerated fictional Events or circumstances, that we can connect with somehow. And this is precisely what Testimony of Miracles will do- it will take you on an eye-opening journey, that is real connective, and spiritual.

TESTIMONY OF MIRACLES

Testimonies are deeply embedded in our Christian culture, and always has its place in churches, or place of worship. However, as the years rolled on, people are using many different mediums to share their miraculous experiences. Allowing others to become more aware of spiritual miracles, and share sameness in faith. Sharing in this respect is important, as it allows those who have these special experiences to acknowledge, connect, and validate ... Not everyone will experience a personal miracle – it is just the way life is. Some people will experience multiple miracles throughout their life time. Whilst others may just experience one, two, three or perhaps none at all. Nevertheless, it is vital for people who have not yet experienced miracle, to be faithful knowing, as long as there is life, then there is hope for miracles. So, do not be dismayed!

Miracle is embedded deeply in the premise of Jehovah Jireh's work. The bible most certainly, highlight many of these events, of which Christians used as references. And so, it is impossible to believe in God, and not believe in miracles. As a Christians, I am no stranger to listing and sharing testimonies. I have been doing this for so many years, it becomes a part of my life. Sharing testimonies of miracles, bring forth a great depth of healing, satisfaction, and togetherness. But a significant phenomenon in all this, is power – the sort of power, you do not feel otherwise. This spiritual power, is the influential source present in any miraculous occurrence – which brings us closer to God. Power is the force behind our life changing decisions, after a miracle. However, it goes without saying, most testimonies of miracles are personal. This might be one of the reasons they are so impacting, we can listen and feel the effect of people's miraculous experiences.

It is fair to say, not all testimonies have an element of miracle. However, they are no less amazing. Quite frequently, especially during church services, people love sharing their general testimonies. And nearly always, they are incredibly amazing. Nevertheless, testimony of miracles somewhat stays with you – it left it marks on you possibly for a life time. This may be because, miracles are hoped for, but they are not expected. If we have got to expect a miracle for something, then its occurrence is more of a favour. And this is what makes miracles so special, interesting, and mysterious.

Time for miracles?

Miracles happen in God's time, as a way of demonstrating his extraordinary presence, and unlimited will- power. It is so, so that people may be able to recognize his work, and whole-heartedly glorify him-as well as strive for closer, and deeper spiritual connection. Miracles are very special, and with every miracle, there is hope for new realization. God is doing something out of the ordinary for our betterment.

Biblical illustration of miracles

The bible has illustrated much of Jesus's miracles, from multiplying five loaves of bread and two fishes and fed five-thousand people; parting the red sea for Moses to cross; and raising Lazarus from the dead. Luke chapter 8 demonstrates various miracles, and evidence of God's devotion to healing and making whole. Jesus is the truth and the light – and through him, we can understand the effectiveness of true miracle. Miracles can be truly eye opening, especially when we are receptive to their occurrences.

Jesus's miracles – healing of the blind man

Jesus was passing by (when he was physically among men) and he saw a blind man, who was born blind. Peter, one of Jesus's disciple, asked why this man was born blind – and whether the man or his parents did sinful things. Jesus explained, neither the man nor his parents had done anything wrong. He was born blind to fulfil God's purpose. He will be healed, and everyone will see, God's miraculous work being manifested ... Jesus spat on the ground, and combined his saliva with clay – created a paste like mixture, and then use it to anoint the blind man's eyes. A short moment after, Jesus sent blind man to wash in the pool of Si-loam. The blind man obeyed, and did just what he was told. On his return, he was no longer blind. Everyone was surprised, those who had witness this miracle, and those who did not, but was then able to acknowledge a blind man, had perfect sight (John 9).

Jesus's miracle – woman with 18 years infirmity

On a sabbath day, Jesus was teaching in one of the synagogues. And in the midst, was a woman who had 18 years of infirmity. Everyone had bow down for a moment, and again stood up after, except this woman who was unable to get back up. When Jesus had laid his hands on her, and she was instantly able to stand straight and walk. She was amazed of her miracle, and immediately glorified God, for his wonderous work (Luke 13).

Jesus's miracle – healing the paralysed man

One day, a very faithful centurion went to see Jesus in Capernaum, and asked him for his help. He told Jesus, there was a sick man – a servant, who was paralysed and tormented with grief. This man was at the centurion's house, hoping for a miracle. Jesus did not hesitate, and told the centurion, alright, I will come ... But the centurion did not feel worthy of Jesus's visit to his house. And in response, he told Jesus, not to go to his house, but instead speak words of healing for this man, from where he was. Jesus humbly did as the centurion asked, and assured him, it was done. Jesus was marvelled by the centurion's faith, and expressed his amazement, as he had not seen such faith amongst the people of Israel (Matthew 8).

Testimony of Miracle

MIRACLE

God works everyday – loving, caring, healing and providing,
Though, the details of his doing are not always visible,

A miracle might not be far away.

I know, life something appears to be a test, But trust God,
as he always gives his best He holds all the power,
So, let him in, and he will bless you with a lifetime of treasures.

And if it takes time, to receive things asked for,
Do not worry, just remain in tune with him,
He may need to move some barriers,
before opening your miracle door.

FEBRUARY 2017

Over the years, I was always returning to Jamaica for a slice of paradise. My visits were mainly for holidays, and of course, and of course, a good old catch-up with friends and family. But there is one year in particular, which was a little exceptional – let us call it very memorable. I had a personal experience, I never even thought would have happened to me. As I do when I am on holiday, I relax … One day, I was lying down on my bed, with pure wandering thoughts – nothing special, to be honest. Then, I suddenly had a thought to check my breasts. I did so, and to my surprise, I had found a lump bigger than a table tennis ball in my left breast. I instantly felt a rush of overwhelming emotions, and went into the next room to seek out my mum's advice. My mum bravely felt my breasts, and when she felt the lump, I saw a change in her facial expression. For some reason, I did not feel scared; instead, I went to the cabinet in the bathroom, and got a bottle of olive oil. I anointed my breast, whilst my mum prayed for me. And as faith is the assurance of things hoped for, and the evidence of things not seen (Hebrews 11: 1), I believed in the power of healing.

Eventually, my mum wanted to know what my decision might be, whether I would go and see a doctor or not. I told her no, I would not accept a doctor prophesying over me. I had already known the importance of exercising faith. Even if my faith is as small as a mustard seed, there is power – this concept, I certainly applied to my life and circumstance. I timely developed a routine based on Christian traditions – where I constantly anointed my breast with consecrated olive oil, for quite some time. This, alongside praying unceasingly and reading Isaiah 54:17 repetitively. Another biblical scripture I had personalized for comfort, was Isaiah 53:5 – Christ was wounded for my transgressions, and bruised for my iniquities, the chastisement of my peace was upon him; and with his stripes, I am healed. I continued to pray for my breast, hoping and trusting God to allow the lump to disappear, without any further effect.

I constantly brought myself to a special place, to connect deeper and deeper with Jesus Christ. Daily embracing strong faith in whom I believe, I know my anchor was always present. Eventually, I decided to share what was happening with my niece – we are very close. Knowing the prayer warrior, she is, together we embarked on a prayer chain. After quite some time, my niece asked whether I was feeling any pain in my breast. I told her not. She explained, she had an unusual experience; whilst she was praying for my breast. She started having terrible intense back pain; and was laid up in bed for many days. My niece thought these circumstances were spiritually related, and decided not to pray with me again. I did not feel disappointed or upset. I was more concerned about my wellbeing – and hoped for her to be alright. I respected her decision. Though I continued my prayer routine, on my own.

Three days later, my niece visited me. She told me God gave her a message for me. She quite sincerely emphasized, God sent her back to pray and anoint my breast for three consecutive days. And once this period passed, the lump should be gone. And that I should not examined my breast. I was obedient to the word of God, and permitted her to do what God had ordained … Some time had passed, and the lump went away indeed. I do not know precisely when it disappeared, but I was grateful to be lump - free. Many year later, I received a letter from my local hospital to attend an appointment for a mammogram. And on this occasion, I destroyed it – my faith in God still stands. I few weeks later, I received another appointment from another hospital with an appointment date, for me to visit the hospital for a mammogram, as I had not kept the previous appointment. I took the letter into my kitchen and burnt it. My faith in God still stands. I trust him explicitly, to take care of me. The word of the Lord is pure and true, and He never goes back on His words.

My experience is the epitome of a true miracle, which is engraved in my memory, and I will forever be grateful and faithful to God. God almighty, is worthy, worthy of all my praises.

DO NOT BE DISMAYED, IF TODAY DOES NOT BRING YOU A SPECIAL MIRACLE – TOMORROW MAY BE YOUR TURN.

Have you shared your story?

Did your miracle bring forth changes?

Have you ever seen someone else experienced a miracle?

What was your thought?

Did it have an effect on your life?

Be confident and share your testimony of miracles, if you have one.

**LET'S GET
STARTED WITH MY PERSONAL TESTIMONY OF MIRACLES!**

SCAR UNDER MY LEFT BREAST

When I found, the lump in my left breast 2017, and I was told by my niece. What God had told her to tell me. That I should not search for the lump. I held unto the word of God. And after my shower I would just apply my body lotion, but I was never tempted, to look at my breast or examined it. On Friday the 3rd of September 2021 I was lotion my body the usual way, and for some unknown, reason I lift my left breast and saw a scar. I found the scar a few days before manuscript was due to be sent to the publisher. This miracle, would not be completed without the evidence of God's amazing miracle. I am allowing a photograph of my scar to be published.

It is impossible to have a scar this size without any discomfort. This is truly a miracle.

Testimony of Miracle

MIRACLE DIARY

Let your miracle story, effectively shine with a miracle diary. Maybe you have some experiences, you have not yet considered as miraculous. And perhaps, they are indeed not miracles – But by reflecting and writing, there could be new realization – your experiences were not ordinary occurrences…

Testimony of Miracle

SUMMER 2006

I had just finished my late shift at a London hospital, and made my way to the bus stop. There were several of us nurses, stood waiting for the bus on the hospital grounds. Suddenly, a car drove up and stopped in front of us, then the driver let out a passenger – it was an old man. The driver came closed, and asked us kindly to help this 91 – year – old man to get to Edmonton Green (London). And of course, we could not say no – all agreed. We got talking with the old man, and he told us, he was at the hospital all day visiting his wife. She was an inpatient on the psychiatric ward. However, he had missed the time, and stayed at the hospital until late. A staff had noticed he was there the entire time, so she asked him nicely to leave. He slowly walked out of the hospital, and a very kind taxi driver gave him a lift to the bus stop. From here on, he was in our care … I had a great deal of empathy for the old man, and decided to make certain he got on the bus to Edmonton Green. But his home was in Hackney, so would need to get on a couple of buses for his journey. I told the other nurses, when we get to Edmonton Green, I would get a taxi to take him home – and for sure, I hoped to pay his fare. However, when we got to Edmonton Green, there was no taxi, and the taxi office was closed. Another decision Had to be made, as his safety was utmost important indeed.

We all got on the bus and travelled to Tottenham. Once we were there, one of the nurses went to get a taxi for the old man. The rest of us went into a café, so the old man could sit down. He asked me for a cigarette, but one of the nurses gave him two. He lit one and put the other in his pocket. A while later, all the nurses except for the one who went to get the taxi, decided that it was time for them to go home. It was getting late, and they had an early start next morning. But before they went, they contributed towards our taxi fare. The old man and I were left alone waiting … We waited some more, until the other nurse came back with a taxi. She gave him another two cigarettes, and apologized for not financially able to help pay the taxi fare. I assured her it was alright, as myself and the other nurses had covered it.

The old man and I got into the taxi, and off we went to Hackney. On approach, the driver asked where in Hackney he was going. The old man responded, he needed to be on the farther side of Hackney. This was miles away from where we were. At that point, I was tired and hoping to be in bed. I could not stop thinking about all the other nurses, already home and resting peacefully in their beds. I generally got home about 10 pm, but this night, I concluded in my mind, I probably will not be at home before midnight. I knew this old man was my priority, and I had to do right by him – and tried hard not to say a word, about my own feelings. The old man was conversing with the driver, and shared his love for West Ham United football club. The conversation appeared delightful, as they chatted about 1966 world cup, England won. Their conversation went on and on for ages. All I was thinking of, was getting home, a good night sleep, and be up early the next morning for work. I usually got on the first bus, at 5 :55am.

Finally, we reached our destination! I then realized, he was living in a residential home. The driver helped the old man out of the taxi. And just before he was on his way home, he asked for a lighter, to light his last cigarette. The driver gave him a lighter – he lit his cigarette and walked towards his home. Once he was finished smoking, he rang the doorbell, and waited for someone to open the door. We made sure he was home safely, before we left. By this time, I was extremely exhausted. I could not help but thinking a day off work, next morning. I know, working without being fully rejuvenated, would only put patients' lives at risk. There is no way, I would be able to think straight…

Time checked – it was nearly midnight! I asked the taxi driver to drive me home – and he did. Phew! Finally, next stop would be mine – home sweet home. The driver was very patient and kind, and had surprised me when I got to my destination, by not charging the full fare - £12 it was for all that journey, which should have been significantly more. However, I got in and straight away check the time – my clock was showing the time as 10pm. I could not believe my eyes, that was impossible! How could I get home the same time, I normally would after a late shift, whilst I spent hours out, after work? This was definitely my miracle time! I know God had stopped the time for me, that I may carry out a good will. I maintained my nightly routine, and went to bed. I had the same hours of sleep, I would usually

have, the next day. I was again fully charged, and ready for work. I have always have faith in God, but on this occasion, my faith in God significantly increased. God is great all the time, and all the time, God is great!

NO MATTER IF,
LIFE CIRCUMSTANCES VARY.

There are miracles out there, for everyone to see,

Just open your eyes, and consider the natural wonders present every day, Some we take for granted, and others, we let be.
There are miracles, which lie deep within, Like love and forgiveness, we cannot explain, Let us give thanks for such a thing- miracle, As sometimes, it takes us out of our misery, And ease our troublesome pain.

Miracles happened every day, sometimes we do not think of them as miracles, Or even recognized them at all. And for sure, the miracles which enable us to give testimonies, Are the ones which are more touching. Perhaps, this is because they are not obvious for everyone to see, unless it is shared. People experienced personal miracles, much more than we know, and have become more hopeful and confident, as a result. There are not many other things, which are more awesome than the power of miracles, which goes completely against all-natural laws – this is phenomenal!

Jesus never ceased to work wonders, and miracles are special wonders. When Jesus distinctively manifests his power – and miracles happen, it is fundamental! And there is an instant feeling and awareness of what it really is – it is the case, where one does not need to even question whether it is a miracle or not – it is beyond human mediums. Miracles are incredible eventualities, which are significantly life changing. And it is time we see them for what they are.

ON MY WAY TO WORK

It was on the 12th of July 2005, and I was on my way to work, the time was 5: 45 am. My journey to work was by public transport (bus). I arrived at the pedestrian crossing at 5: 50 am and I did the usual, look right and left and right again – there was no vehicle on the road, so I quickly crossed the road. As I crossed the road and put my feet on the pavement a car appeared from nowhere and came straight at me, I just felt someone give me one big push in my back and it was that push which saved my life. When I got over the shock the distance between myself and the car was no distance, and that was the day which I faced death straight in my face. There was no one at the bust stop and there was no one around. However, someone saved my life THANK YOU JESUS.

GLASS OF WATER FROM THE TOP (PIPE)

I can remember this clearly. It was one morning in May 2014, I cannot remember the exact day or date. However, this was what happened, it came into my spirit that I should get a glass of water, from the top (pipe) not bottle water and pray over it and drink it first thing in the morning. I followed my spirit and just did that for a few mornings. On the 4th morning I felt something in my throat, but nothing came up. However, on the 5th morning I was woken with something in my throat blocking it. I got out of bed quickly and ran to the bathroom and got some tissue and spat on the tissue and I could not believe what came out of my throat, a big piece of white flesh. The only way in which I can describe it, is like when white fat is cleaned off the meat only this was not fat it was flesh. From that day I make it a point of duty every morning. The first thing I would do is to get my glass of water prayed over it and drink it.

These are the days of the fulfillment of the book of REVELATION in our lives. This book of REVELATION is not just for Christians but it is for the world. Have all the pastors in the world who claim that they are children of God who also claimed that they were called by God have they taken and read the seven letters which was sent to them? I only hope and pray that they have. I also prayed that all the pastors would go into a season of prayer and fasting for the end is near. Where are the John the Baptist of today? Are you out of the wilderness and crying to the world? Telling the world that the Kingdom of Heaven is at hand prepare yourself to meet your maker? Will you be taking one soul into the kingdom with you? Please remember what Jehovah said that the church is not holy and that the pastors are filthy rags. We should all get ourselves in order and I am included in this. We must be ready for his coming.

There is also another scripture which I would like to share with you which is also linked with the book of REVELATION. And I would like to share it with you.

2 CHRONICLES chapter 7 v 14

If my people, which are called by my name, shall humble themselves, and pray, and seek my face, and turn from their wicked ways; then will I hear from heaven, and will forgive their sin, and will heal their land.

2 CHRONICLES chapter 7 V 15

Now mine eyes shall be open, and mine ears attend unto the prayer that is made in this place.

2 CHRONICLES chapter 7 V 16

For now I have chosen and sanctified this house, that my name may be there forever; and mine ears and my heart shall be there perpetually.

2 CHRONICLES chapter 7 V 17

And as for thee, if thou will walk before me, as David thy father walked, and do according to all that I have commanded thee, and shalt observe my statutes and my judgement;

2 CHRONICLES chapter 7 V 18

Then will I stablish the throne of thy kingdom, according as I have covenanted with David thy father, saying, There shall not fail thee a man to be ruler in Israel.

2 CHRONICLES chapter 7 v 19

But if ye turn away, and forsake my statutes and my commandments, which I have set before you, and shall go and serve other gods, and worship them.

2 CHRONICLES chapter 7 v 20

Then will I pluck them up by the roots out of my land which I have given them; and this house which I have sanctified for my name, will I cast out of my sight, and will make it to be a proverb and a byword among all nations.

2 CHRONICLES chapter 7 v 21

This house, which is high, shall be an astonishment to everyone that passeth by it; so that he shall say, Why hath the LORD done thus unto this land, and unto this house?

2 CHRONICLES chapter 7 V 22

And it shall be answered, Because they forsook the LORD God of their fathers, which brought them forth out of the land of Egypt, and laid hold on other gods, and worshipped them, and served them: therefore hath he brought all this evil upon them.

Are we still in bondage to sin/ has sin taken over our life? Are we has Christians denied our calling come of our road to JESUS CHRIST and on the road to hell. We should all remember that in the end Satan will not be in charge of hell because JESUS has already taken the keys of death and hell, which simple means that Satan has no power over hell. Because he himself will be in the lake of fire for all eternity.

After reading the book of REVELATION chapter 2 &3 and 2 CHRONICLES 7 we can see for ourselves that JEHOVAH leave us his laws and his commandments that we has children of GOD should follow in his laws and his commandments. It is only by following JEHOVA'S LAWS AND HIS COMMANDMENTS we can enter into the Kingdom of Heaven.

THE SERMON ON THE MOUNT

MATTHEW chapter 5 V 1

Ans seeing the multitudes, he went up into a mountain: and when he was set, his disciples came unto him:

MATTHEW chapter 5 V 2

And he opened his mouth, and taught them, saying,

MATTHEW chapter 5 v 3

Blessed are the poor in spirit: for theirs is the Kingdom of heaven.

MATTHEW chapter 5 v 4

Blessed are they that mourn: for they shall be comforted.

MATTHEW chapter 5 v 5

Blessed are the meek: for they shall inherit the earth.

MATTHEW chapter 5 v 6

Blessed are they which do hunger and thirst after righteousness: for they shall be filled.

MATTHEW chapter 5 v 7

Blessed are the merciful; for they shall obtain mercy.

MATTHEW chapter 5 V 8

Blessed are the pure in heart; for they shall see GOD.

MATTHEW chapter 5 v 9

Blessed are the peacemaker: for they shall be called the children of God.

MATTHEW chapter 5 v 10

Blessed are they which are persecuted for 'righteousness sake; for theirs is the kingdom of heaven.

MATTHEW chapter 5 v 11

Blessed are ye, when men shall revile you, and persecute you, and shall say all manner of evil against you falsely, for my sake.

MATTHEW chapter 5 v 12

"Rejoice, and be exceeding glad: for great is your reward in heaven: for so persecuted they the prophets which were before you.

MATTHEW chapter 5 v 13

Ye are the salt of the earth; but if the salt have lost his savour, wherewith shall it be salted? It is thenceforth good for nothing, but to be cast out, and to be trodden under the foot of men.

MATTHEW chapter 5 v 14

Ye are the light of the world, A city that is set on a hill cannot be hid.

MATTHEW chapter 5 v 15

Neither do men light a candle and put it under a bushel, but on a candlestick; and it giveth light unto all that are in the house.

MATTHEW chapter 5 v 16

Let your light so shine before men, that they may see your good works, and glorify your father which is in heaven.

MATTHEW chapter 5 v 17

Think not that I am come to destroy the law, or the prophets: I am not come to destroy but to fulfil.

MATTHEW chapter 5 v 18

For verily I say unto you, Till heaven and earth pass, one jot or one tittle shall in no wise from the law, till all be fulfilled.

MATTHEW chapter 5 v 19

Whosever therefore shall break one of these least commandments, and shall teach men so, he shall be called the least in the kingdom of heaven: but whosoever shall do and teach them, the same shall be called great in the kingdom of heaven.

MATTHEW chapter 5 v 20

For I say unto you, That except your righteousness shall exceed the righteousness of the scribe and Pharisees, ye shall in no case enter into the kingdom of heaven.

MATTHEW CHAPTER 5 V 21

Ye have heard that it was said by them of old time, Thou shalt not kill; and whosoever shall kill shall be in the danger of the judgement:

MATTHEW chapter 5 v 22

But I say unto you, that whosoever is angry with his brother without a cause shall be in danger of the judgement: And whosoever shall say to his brother, Raca, shall be in danger of the council: but whosoever shall say, Thou fool, shall be in danger of hell fire.

MATTHEW chapter 5 v 23

Therefore if thou bring thy gift to the alter, and there rememberest that thy brother ought against thee;

MATTHEW chapter 5 v 24

Leave there thy gift before the alter, and go thy way; first be reconciled to thy brother, and then come and offer thy gift.

MATTHEW chapter 5 v 25

Agree with thine adversary quickly, whiles thou art in the way with him; lest at any time the adversary deliver thee to the judge, and the judge deliver thee to the officer, and thou be cast into prison.

MATTHEW chapter 5 V 26

Verily I say unto thee, Thou shall by no means come out thence, till thou hast paid the uttermost farthing.

MATTHEW chapter 5 v 27

Ye have heard that it has was said by them of old time, Thou shalt not commit adultery:

MATTHEW chapter 5 v 28

But I say unto you, That whosoever looketh on a woman to lust after her hath committed adultery with her already in his heart.

MATTHEW chapter 5 v 29

And if thy right eye offended thee, pluck it out, and cast it from thee: for it is profitable for thee that one of thy members should perish, and not that thy whole body should be cast into hell.

MATTHEW chapter 5 v 30

And if thy right hand offend thee, cut it off, and cast it from thee: for it is profitable for thee that one of thy members should perish, and not that thy whole body should be cast into hell.

MATTHEW chapter 5 v 31

It hath been said, Whosever shall put away his wife, let him give her a writing of divorcement:

MATTHEW chapter 5 v 32

But I say unto you, That whosoever shall put away his wife, saving for the cause of fornication, causeth he to commit adultery: and whosoever shall marry her that is divorced committeth adultery.

MATTHEW chapter 5 v 33

Again, ye have heard that it hath bee said by them of old time, Thou shall not forswear thyself, but shall perform unto the Lord thine oaths:

We can all see the book of REVELATION fulfilling in the churches to day.

When JEHOVAH spoke to me on the 7th of July 2021, he said the churches is not holy and the pastors of the church are filthy rags. We must therefore ask ourselves where are we in GOD. Have the pastors of the churches read the 7 letters which was sent out to the churches.

There is something extraordinary about sharing – especially sharing personal experiences, which are deeply touching. This may be because it reflects real situations, rather than exaggerated fictional events or circumstances, that we can connect with somehow. And this is precisely what Testimony of Miracles will do- it will take you on an eye-opening journey, that is real connective, and spiritual.

WHEN DO I ASK FOR A MIRACLE?

Well, let us face facts, whenever everything is going swimmingly well, we just fill our hearts with contentment. In that case, a miracle would not necessarily be on our minds. Most times, when I am in a position where I need a miracle, it is fair to say, I might not be having the positive experience. I may be feeling helpless, hopeless, distraught, or even traumatised... The life scale is definitely at a tipping point, in quite an unbalanced way – if I need a miracle. But regardless of my desperate aspiration for a miracle, it is quite a sure thing, I do not always get one ... As well as, I could get such a miracle aspired for, but not at the time when I am anticipating it. Yet when I received it, it feels like the perfect time for it to happened. In those moments, everything that is right feels great – like a perfect alignment, or difficult jig saw puzzles that come together perfectly.

WHO DO I ASK FOR A MIRACLE?

I only look to God for my miracles – if it is not from God, it is not from God it is certainly is not a miracle. For this reason, I am forever giving God praises for the wonderful miraculous experiences, I have had. Without them, I know for sure, my life would have been different. And I mean, different in a less positive way. My miraculous experiences shaped my life, my decisions, my choice and impact my life-path significantly. They allow me to grow from strength to strength, with more resilience to face everyday challenges. There ls no doubt, that my experiences in this respect, keep my eyes focused on God always.

Testimony of Miracle

GRATITUDE

Many people enjoy showing gratitude for their miracles – whatever they may be. And of course, the ultimate way, is to glorify God in spirit and in truth – and maintain that connection. Though other common ways may include encouraging and uplifting others, especially when their faces are towards the ground, and it seems all hope is gone.

POETRY

MIRACLE UNQUESTIONABLE

Miracles are unquestionable eventualities,
Their occurrences are apparent,
And you know, there should be no doubting God's powerful abilities.

He makes no secrets of his divinity, He said trust me inwardly,
And I will reward you openly.

So, when you see his power in action,

Lots of shares, smiles and praises – should be your reaction.

God is holy, powerful, and magnificent beyond our greatest
imaginations, And miracles he will serve,
without barriers and distractions.

Testimony of Miracle

A PRAYER

Father in heaven, I seek you now, At your feet, I humbly bow.
You alone, knows my heart, There is nothing that you cannot see,
Keep me close, that that we will never be a part. Quite often,
I let myself strayed from your words
But Dear Father, please restore faith in me
That my life will align with your way, as one accord.

Holy one above, today, this is my plea, So please humble me.

Let me hear your voice, oh Lord …
As words spoken, will be my light …

IN GOD'S LOVE

Shine your love upon me,
Brightly, that all may see.
Let your blessings flow through me,
And all the things I may do to please Thee.
Let my kindness, touch the hearts of many,
And your work, I will continue to do beautifully.

Testimony of Miracle

HUMBLE PRAYER

Father, let me connect with you through faith,

Teach me thy ways, that I may seek you before embracing my desires.

Let my worship be from my heart,
Filled with prayerful words, Whilst you direct my daily paths.
And if my prayers are lacking … Teach me how to improve,
That I may stay stronger in you, and not be moved.

Testimony of Miracle

CHRISTIAN ME

Being a Christian made me who I am, today,
Kept me grounded, as the Dear Lord, paved my way.
The doctrine reminds me, to be sweet and kind,

And regardless of differences, we were all gifted wonderful minds.

The godliness in me, I try to show,

I hope my life is a beacon, that certainly glows.

Being a Christian, is a wonderful thing, you know,
So, I hope today, you will find Christ, and in him you will grow.

Testimony of Miracle

DEAR JEHOVAH

Your love is so patient and kind,
Embed your love in my heart,
Let me be meek and gentle, like a child.

Blessed my body with such strength,
That I may endure life's challenges,
And embrace situational changes.

Testimony of Miracle

GOD'S GUIDANCE

I pray for guidance and strength each day, Lest,
I rely on my own will and stray.
Teach me Father, to be kind, Because it is your will and not mine.
Please let me continuously seek thy face,
It is the only place, that I find saving grace.
I pray you dwell, more in me,
Dear Lord, as I pray these simple words on Thee.

LET ME LISTEN ...

Let me listen to your still voice,
That you may guide me through the darkest night,
Father I thank you, for been my Father, and for the special,
Love which you have for me, that you send your son Jesus Christ,
To be my sacrificial Lamb,
Thank you Father.

SEEK YOUR MIRACLE

Do not close your mind-eyes and give up just yet,
Life is tough, for sure,
And everything seems like a test
Some days you afford a half smile,
Other days, hopelessness is paramount,
Enough to pave the royal mile.
But prayer is a tool we use to open doors,
Trust in God, and you will see, The miracles, he can let be.

Maybe you will need to wait a while,
And it is worth being patient,
Knowing great things only done in God's time
And when his favour is upon you,
His grace you will find. All will fall into place.
And your perfect miracle will be just right,
Praises will be given to God, for His saving grace.

Testimony of Miracle

MIRACLE IS EXTRAORDINARY

Miracles from God are not rare,
But when they present, worries disappear.
There effects are stronger than words can say,
And the amazement they bring, aids godly connections,
For sure, they are evident in our existence every day.
Miracles are extraordinary,
And can happen to anyone, and at any time.

MIRACLES

God work every day – loving, caring, healing, and providing.
Through, the details of his doings are not always visible,
A miracle might not be far away.
I know, life sometime appears to be a test,
But trust in God, as he always give his best.
He holds all the power,
So, let him in, and he will bless you with a life time of treasures.
And if it takes some time, to receive things asked for,
Do not worry, just remain in tune with him,
He may need to move some barriers,
before opening your miracle door.

Testimony of Miracle

THANK YOU

Thank you for loving me through and through,
Thank you, for standing by me, when I am very low,
Thank you, for every support you have given me,
And I thank God, for allowing me to have you
… Just want to remind you, I love you too.

Woman who had 12 years bleeding issue Matthew 5:25

The man with dropsy Luke 14

Jesus feed the four thousand Mark 8

Healing of Peter's mother in law Matthew 8:14-15

… Walking on water Matthew 14:22-33

Healing the deaf Mark 7:31-37

Jesus cures a leper Mark 1:40

Jesus calms the sea Matthew 8: 23 - 27